The Grand Complication

© 2019 by Devin King

Published by Kenning Editions
3147 W Logan Blvd., Suite 7, Chicago, IL 60647

Kenningeditions.com

Distributed by Small Press Distribution
1341 Seventh St., Berkeley, CA 94710

Spdbooks.org

ISBN: 978-0-9997198-5-5
Library of Congress Control Number: 2018915294

Cover design by Crisis
Interior composition by Patrick Durgin

A portion of Volume One was published in Issue One of *Aurochs*. Many thanks to Stephen Williams.

This book was made possible in part by the supporters of Kenning Editions: Charles Bernstein, Julietta Cheung, Joel Craig, Craig Dworkin, Jais Gossman, Judith Goldman, Rob Halpern, Lyn Hejinian, Joshua Hoglund, Brenda Iijima, Kevin Killian, Rodney Koeneke, Adalaide Morris, Caroline Picard, Barbara Troolin, Anna Vitale, and Tyrone Williams.

Kenning Editions is a 501c3 non-profit, independent literary publisher investigating the relationships of aesthetic quality to political commitment. Consider donating or subscribing: Kenningeditions.com/shop/donation

The Grand Complication

Devin King

11
Vol. 1: The Temple

35
Vol. 2: The Dialogue of the Two Twins

55
Vol. 3: The Body

*...das Geheimnis der Liebe ist größer
als das Geheimnis des Todes.*

Strauss/Lachmann/Wilde

Vol. 1: The Temple
Argument

The Oedipal Curse—Eteocles Banishes Polynices—Wandering Polynices—Polynices Happens Upon The Temple—Polynices and Tydeus in Bed—William and Marion in Bed—A Couple Plans—William and Marion Walk to Work—Headphones—Garcia Blocks a Play—Two Lovers Under a Stage—King Adrastus Finds Polynices and Tydeus—The King Recognizes an Omen's Fulfillment—Polynices and Tydeus Worship and Marry—Marion at Phil's Bar—Mike, The Cad—Mike and Julia Flirt—Marion Begins to Plan—Costume Night at Videoland—William, Painted Silver—Garcia Drives Home—Kieron and Deray get Beer—William Locks Up

I.

Thebes' double family parenting sins:
two daughters, sons. Their complete
memories make my incomplete sight
strong, so inward eyes probed
sing chasms Oedipus's scabs invent.

Spring's dark rain gods pierce
darker winter's imagination. Rivers overflow
moving rivers the frozen ground
cannot absorb. So too Tisiphone,
snake-locked Fury, seeds evil.

Patriarchal Oedipus is in decline.
No more mistaken death, unions.
Now every act is understood,
destiny is replaced by reason.
Brothers alternate statecraft's yearly obedience.

But Eteocles in power weeps,
sick with knowledge of responsibility
unenforceable by incestuous Oedipal signature.
No father's brother rules easily,
a king needs a sphinx.

Myth invented war, reason steals
from myth doubling its evil.
Incomplete power hates incomplete power
so Eteocles blames his brother
for his own failed legislation.

What else can he do?
The only unity possible: blame.
Eteocles makes public private hatred,
his family drama goes national,
Polynices will be forever exiled.

II.

Wandering Polynices sees Phoebus blink,
Diana blossom and hush, then
dart and roll to cover
Earth in hard won dream
but twilight rays double back.

Diana watches mixed pictures mean
nothing. Images left are broken,
their changing form molded useless.
Darkness within, darkness without but
my breath makes Polynices' sound.

Blind Polynices remembers his father.
He ignores the armed shadows.
Fire. He sees a temple.
It is old, unused, empty.
Straw bed in the corner.

Suddenly darkness touches two bodies
with weary urgency as Tydeus,
small but strong and wet
with travel, conforms his body.
New brothers share a dream.

III.

Even the night reveals hollies
framing a central Texas window
that contains a couple's crescendo.
William revolves and Marion's delight
appears healthy blush above white.
Now their distance matches yours
and mine. May the cure
come from these various follies.

Kohlrabi meows and Marion lifts
herself up. Checks phone, emails.
"I think I'm gonna bail."
"Ok." "Wanna smoke some weed?"
Grabs joint, phone, checks feed.
"No thanks." Break-up in degrees.
"Back after work with Chinese?"
"Nah, I'm covering a shift."

She walks to Phil's bar,
he splits to the Videoland
staffed by kids in bands.
"Meet after at The Complex?"
 His apartment, the usual suspects.
"K, but I'm gonna be pissy."
"What better fix than whisky?"
"Fucking Julia, Ms. Future Filmstar."

IV.

Marion puts in her headphones
and chooses songs by mood.
Gloom: Micachu, *Chopped and Screwed*.
Understands she'll never kiss him
browsing her library's menu system.
She plays *Hounds of Love*
and then *Hand in Glove*.
Feel better playlist: LedZep Clones.

William misunderstands loss in variance.
A few minutes of *Bongripper*,
Dr. John, the Night Tripper.
Frank Sinatra's *No One Cares*,
The Misfits, *Where Eagles Dare*.
Then Träd, Gräs, och Stenar,
Cars, *Fast Car*, Big Star.
Each random song is luxuriant.

V.

William walks by the converted warehouses.
Half-open door welcomes bugs to the rehearsal.
Two breaths hold as Garcia stops, blocks above them.
Upstage Gilberto and Jesse unroll green turf,
cover aging red of painted stage. It is warm.

The director speaks: "Alright! The grownups have left
so you can begin to make lazy eye contact.
You are each internally satisfied, worried
about your lover, friend, so offer up your own dream.
Double yourself for yourself and for your selves."

Each of the four lovers' laughs at the fifth loosens
the others. But they are quickly professional.
Young bodies diffuse vibration as they settle
into places. Then a slight quiet, a secret nod.
They grope to the scene's present interpretation.

Jesse touches Gilberto's wrist. They drop their work
to watch. The voices carry forwards and remain
unheard. What can be seen in the body's effort?
If it is not yet joined to distinction how can
descriptive song be well-crafted? Moving thought moves.
Rehearsal presents truth in successive glamours.

VI.

We turn towards actors' bodies. Two become four
through attention and in a fifth intentions fuse
currents. Integrity hides in encrusted lamps
whose present surface presents an object's present:
twinkling presence unified in space performed.

From behind, Deray's concrete shadow anchors
in diagonal slash the plump silent distance
to the doubled Chelsea, hand to knee, opposite
foot extended in dancer's flat. The eye connects
her pointedness to her shoulder's pink joint release,
for Julia's fond hand unites attraction's twin
and Julia's left ear puckered by invisible
smile seen under right eye lifted into right brow
fulfills Kieron, upright, leaning away. Pleasure.

Now see the V reversed through Garcia's brown eyes
become an M, then two I's. He stops them.
"Don't separate so totally. These loves are paired.
The marriages are meant democratically-
a slow dispersal of individual choice."

He watches them try and fail again. "K, you've pulled
in too far but this..." points, Deray's hand, pocket. "How?"
The actor's reduction and reversal contains
no arch cynicism in its repetition.
How does Deray know vertical time? Become one.

And in this oneness gestures made strange makes sense.
Hermetic dualists say action joins intention
but in thinking gestures action's thought embodies.
Deray's body making now made makes Deray join
three or four or five (more?) instrumental himselves.

Unity does not number a series of states
but states numerous unities hiding from time.
Expression reveals and binds time to history

so the mind, dumb unextended protuberance,
is allowed an imaginative performance.

So myth is made from the body's jealous mind. Siblings
forever joined each performing still thought we see
moving, moved by a world filled with other objects
inlaid with the same jewels. Why does Deray put his
hand in his pocket and turn his shoulder away?

VII.

All the systems we sit for make artists make now
time new time. Children outside my window given
meaning by me are given meaning where they come
from, where they go. It never ends. So this poem.
I cannot help birthing twins myself, space and time.

And these two twins, body and mind and space and time,
born in spring, give me enough reason to behold
and held might quiet their quaternal confusion.
So go the four lovers only known in tandem.
We cannot complete them yet. Are two ready at hand?

As much as the two stage hands want it (to be them)
four hands already compromise beneath the stage.
Leave future lovers behind for the present love;
unity is only seen in number even
if under number is always another one.

But who is under whom? Which bottom is bottom?
We discover the play where play is most real.
An ass in the hand of the king. Bottom feeling
Oberon's bald crown. Two released from rehearsal
release. What metaphor will be found here? Join me.

VIII.

So much fucking begins...
                              ...Bottom's head is elsewhere,
concrete and distant as the moving May light stains
held by no form in the masterwork held in wide
focus inform the book. Earlier, couch, reading
Bresson, donkey master, past consciousness present.

Imagine I am all face. Two mobile eyes in
mobile head, on a mobile body. An actor
uncertain like uncertain color made from two
tones superimposed. A film bonds persons to each
other, and to objects, by looks. Not artful, agile.

Actor: It's not me you are seeing and hearing,
it's the other man. But being unable to
be wholly the other, he is not that other.
Himself withdrawn. The little he lets escape, take
only what suits you. Don't run after poetry.

The banqueting house. The long house. The disguising
house. Hung with birch and ivy. Garnished with bushels
of roses and honeysuckles from royal gardens.
The chamber. The wardrobe of robes. The removing
wardrobe of beds. No more surface. Instead surfaces,

seized with the desire of pleasing. To bend his head
gracefully to one side, to drop over his eyes,
almond-shaped black deep lids whose lashes, long and bent,
make a brown line over his cheek, to devise tones
that infuse subtle charms into common phrases.

Twenty-one masks. A new cloth of gold, black, and white.
Murrey satin made for a queen. Reading, fucking
knights of the body of Earth's ever still movement
mouth each other's speech so their movement unites
air and matter long thought other now together.

An infinite progression of the trapped, hunted.
Into the breath of related matter is forced
the sensations of romance, collection, and structure.
The breadth where nothing else had. Mint, pea shoots, roe with lime.
See all at a glance, reading desire/body/mind.

IX.

As Bottom finishes rehearsal repeats.
He hears the words but cannot see their containers.
"These things seem small and undistinguishable, like
far-off mountains turned into clouds. Methinks I see
things with parted eye, everything seems double."

"And I have Demetrius like a jewel, mine own,
and not mine own. Are you sure that we are awake?"
"It seems to me that yet we sleep, we dream." "He did
bid us follow to the temple." "We are awake."
"Follow him. By the way, let us recount our dreams."

X.

Morning. King Adrastus, party planner,
inspects the empty, unused temple.
"This will work, with cleanup."
He takes the feast seriously,
understands rule as small rituals.

But the temple is alive.
Sudden movement scares the King
and the boys are terrified
they've broken some unknown rule.
Luckily the exiles are recognized.

Adrastus introduces the bedmates,
The Lion meets The Boar.
A King knows all families
but, even better, knows when
arrival fits into a prophecy.

The feast must begin now.
First he calls for water, soap,
new clothes, fire, and incense.
Clean boys follow Adrastus's prayers,
thank fate for new friendships.

But the King goes on.
Remember, for him ritual's real.
He listens to the omens
that tell him to marry
his daughters to two exiles.

How can they refuse him?
Suddenly the feast's a wedding.
The temple is full again,
even rational actors mythologize fucking.
All toast the King's vision.

XI.

Dart players yell, mark scores,
and the losers buy rounds.
Marion puts on some Townes,
stocks beer, stacks glasses, plates,
cuts limes. Mike arrives late
with a bottle of Pedialyte.
"Must've been a good night."
"Back's weak and prick's sore."

Another night, Marion would respond
but suddenly Julia flops down
waves arms, yells, and frowns
in jokey imitation of rude
customers but, *seriously though, food*.
"These two are on fuego."
"BLT, but hold the tomatoes."
Mike: "Anything for a blonde."

He puts in the order,
asks Julia how rehearsal went
and nods as she vents.
He slags actors he knows.
Marion watches the waitress glow
in appreciation of his slander.
"Someone sexier should play Lysander."
He's making advances towards her.

XII.

"I don't think he wanted
to be a nightingale, Joe-Bob."
William mimes a blow job,
"This again?" He's halfway behind
the counter when Eve binds
his hands, throws him down.
She's dressed as a clown,
there's corpse paint on Ted.

Eve sprays him with bodypaint,
puts dented funnel on head,
stands up and high-fives Ted.
It's costume night at Videoland:
Pennywise, a zombie, the Tin-Man.
"You need a new heart!"
"Motherfuckers, don't you fucking start."
William breaks free from restraint.

XIII.

Marion works while they flirt,
remakes quiet frustration into stoicism.
Mike's silly with filthy lyricism
that arrogantly describes his pants
holding earth's most important inhabitant.
He finally notices Marion's glares
and ends this initial affair.
"Dirty quirt is gonna spurt."

"You're such a fucking asshole."
"What? She's not fucking anybody."
"Beer and a hot toddy."
"You kidding? It's fucking 90."
"Here's your toddy, pint, he's
having a bad night. Dude!
Don't be so fucking crude."
"I'm not crude, I'm droll."

XIV.

Marion works while they flirt,
Garcia waits until everyone's gone,
locks up and walks the parking lot to his bright red
truck looking currant lit only by moon. Drive's short but night's
nice so he takes the long way windows down on low
college station plays *De Natura Sonorum*.

His mind resets into the quiet. Forget play.
Forget actors. Forget sets. Forget music, lights.
Forget stage. Forget curtains. Forget seats, aisles, doors.
Forget lobby. Forget box office, bar, restrooms.
Forget marquee, forget windows, forget theater.

And in the truck's rolling stillness see Garcia
plumb no thing but himself and in himself no thing
known through inward cosmology of given light
but things given only by dramaturgy
that with silver light gives hidden things relation.

What stage could hold all of it? Unfixed memories
spill out in as he pulls the wheel into a turn
he understands a jump rope, sneakers, then pavement.
small points in Apollonian relation, still
Euclidian space given motion by tangents.

So the grey pavement becomes grey smoke pouring out
of his first boyfriend's face whose touch becomes the touch
of a small kitten suddenly grown still, dying
beneath the bed made with ladled cranberry sauce.
The narrative of inward images is now
no more a secret than gravity to the sun.
This director loves himself but wants something more
and aims forgetfulness not only at the world
but at himself. Forget berries. Forget bed, cat.
Forget Eric, his cigarettes, and the jump rope.

And then the larger things that touch both world and self.
For those alone like Garcia forgetting these
is easier, for those alone like you and me
the work is difficult. Why? In the impression
of the self relation can be overlooked but
only when these impressions are understood as
coming into the world with things as other things.
Secret moments—in a truck or underwater—
make these things weightless; economics, religion,
identity...they all can disappear together.
The book's mind, clearly made, cannot be extinguished.
I cannot be forgotten. Homeric escape
(or biblical) is negative enlightenment.
But supposing I could remake myself, vanish.
You'd still be, wondering how this book came to be.

In the truck Parmegiani's tones summon belief.
So does this book. This is depth added to a world
filled with silent, responsive things on a flat plane.
Each real, imagined, relational thing's weight
is then weighed by another and given matter.
Recognition thus given also comes within;
The truck is turned by Garcia and the paved road.
Time's twins—inner freedom (possibility) and
outer fate (destiny) meet in things and so space,
central Texas, rings. The truck pulls into the drive.

XV.

Tender boys jovial after rehearsal, *The Who Sell Out* loud
on the phone plugged into car stereo, Kieron, air drummer,
Deray, left turn across traffic to neon drive-thru liquor store
The Beer Temple. Now arguments of taste using frosty logic
to figure couch change for a tall boy sixer: Lone Star or High Life?

XVI.

Ode to the High Life

past light
suddenly stairs
grant me
new servitude

proliferation
of forms
cancel
out form
turn back
into matter

a muff
corded
in a bundle

Ode to the Lone Star

I asked
to see
all

I asked
what it might
be like

to see
all

so change
was not
me becoming
another

but me
becoming
myself

asking
to witness

asking
to see

whatever
might
be seen

as
myself

as
no one
else

a theatreless
stage

XVII.

"All these years you've been playing me for a sucker. Planting evidence, aiding justice."

William, silver, ends his shift,
cuts off the television, lights.
Might smoke a joint, might
do a lot of things. Locks
up, puts on headphones, walks
mindlessly in the bar's direction.
Time to make a selection.
Presses play: *Red*, Taylor Swift.

Vol. 2: The Dialogue of the Two Twins
Argument

Julia Changes—The Bench Scene, Carousel—Tydeus travels to Thebes—Peace Attempted, Refused—Theban Assassins!—Marion texts William—William, Silver—Marion asks William to Flirt with Julia, Keep Mike Away—William, Confused—Tydeus Kills the Assassins—Garcia Cooks—King Adrastus Calls his Prophets, most notably, Amphiaraus—The Prophecies are, shall we say, Not Good—Four Lovers: Marion, Mike, William, Julia—Garcia goes to sleep, reads Ovid—Two Twins—King Adrastus and Co. March Towards Thebes—Bacchus, Lover of Thebes, Dries up the Rivers—The King's Army, Dying of Thirst—Hypsipyle, Nursing Opheltes—King Adrastus asks Hypsipyle for help—Hypsipyle Leads the Army to a Secret, Underground River: Langia—Deray, Kieron Arrive at The Complex—The Army Drinks, the Child Dies

I.

Julia, of two minds, lets the bar and the double bar
wash over her in the break room changing out of movement
clothes and character shoes into demure black on black made
potent with red kerchief found loose in her branded tote,
quieter, deeper than a well, on repeat The Bench Scene,
sung along with not outward for fear of being found and
interrupted but inward, loud, perspective given to
life by music written for a play no longer studied
in Texas except in relation to a musical
filled with musical hints to the characters' true feelings—
confusion and hopelessness wed to love's freedom only
known through sadism's respite forgiven in after life.

                                          In the woods?

No!

                                          On a beach?

No!

                                          Did you love him?

No, I've never told that to anyone.

Now, without her knowing, you, others, see her listening.
These voices she hears speak of becoming, of finding love.
So then, let her hear you, hear us instead. What will you say?

II.

Tydeus, Adrastus's new Theban proxy
lacks rhetoric: literal olive branch
assures dismissal from Eteocles's court.
A lonely walk in reverse
whose end is likely war.

A valley, two barren cliffs.
Plants, animals remember the sphinx.
New moonlight betrays hidden assassins
sent by the brother king.
Compact Tydeus grunts and flexes.

III.

Marion texts Will on break.
(Subtext is she's cockblocking Mike.)

Come to the bar.
          Like
          ...
          ...
          I'm already here.

Looks up.
His silver form approaches.

          Sup.
The fuck?
          Pretty tight, huh?
Tight?
          I'm the Tin-Man, bruh!
          And I'm on the make.

His sleaze has youth's grace,
but an insouciant silver dandy
no longer makes her randy.
Make way for new love,
always to the new love.
Marion hides change beneath disgust
and explains Mike's vile thrusts.
Stoicism marks a silver face.

She reveals the new norms
and suggests that Will hunt another
to soothe her guilt for transforming her lover.
He's confused. Wants to please.
He sublimates the forced antipodes.
It's quick. She has to get back to work.
No hug, no kiss, she feels like a jerk
without silver on her uniform.

IV.

Tydeus's throat, inwardly useless, easily
deflects the spear now asked
to retrace its last flight
to find its last home.
Shock marks the other men.

Number is their only strategy,
his, faith in his body.
They give up high ground
so he retreats upwards, finds
oversized furniture made of rock.

See the sinewy man lift
the lion bird man's bed.
Four men sleep beneath it.
Two try the javelin trick,
two hands catch, release, kill.

The remaining act as one
but he is one in
the way of them all.
With a dead man's shield
Tydeus catches each last spear.

Rest assured, every foe killed.
But remember this one image
made of five objects by
the bodies of two men:
spear thread jawbone tongue mind.

V.

In self dissent Garcia oils pan, sweats leeks, and adapts
Dürrenmatt's *Romulus*, setting begun on vacation
sitting atop Hawk Tower when a silver-brown ranch house
appeared thrust into the red sea as a focused vision
out of the houses Jeffers's tower was built to ignore.

A '70s Romulus, hip swinging suburban dad,
his Byzantine mirror Zeno as a self-serious
Esalen type and the Teutons just straights from the era.
His mind casts La Razas as assimilating valets,
Aemilian and Rea, peaceniks on adulthood's edge.

Inherited figures present even now to his mind.
How would the play be seen in forty years? A condo in
a gentrified neighborhood? Romulus, programming his
chicken app and Zeno importing Szechuan peppers
for his pop up blackout dinner party? Was this close to

Kott's cruel history blanked to precise absurdity,
or more precise than Brook's blank universal mythmaking?
Two masters in his humble way he hopes to overtake.
Would this be all he added? His own historical count?
His mind wants Nietzsche's Greeks, the clear forms of their deities.

In search of this specific clarity his mind idles.
He adds bread, garlic, a bit more oil, salt, and pepper,
turns up the heat. What deities are at work in this house?
This image the only thing known from the vision on high.
Begin again there then. In this house cast no human roles,

and find in it its own empire and show me, us, how it fell.
What then? The house acts, writes itself as in *To the Lighthouse*?
Any object's possibility seen in performance,
a smile as he adds the asparagus and tomatoes
seeing another history behind his thought, avant-garde
resistance to the subjective whether Marinetti
or Cage, through to L=A=N=G=U=A=G=E and...more historical patterns.

Neither here nor there that image, and through that image mind,
safe and stable on Hawk Tower performing itself in
silver brown thrust into the red sea containing nothing

no humans acting nor itself, symbolic aggragate
presenting itself vortextual origin aware, breathing
in concert with the small coterie assembled at the
Central Texas warehouse home to Garcia's small theater
where Romulus will never be played, except in his mind.

With all your heart?

                                            With all my heart.

You would do anything I ask you?

                                            I will do anything.

You would take a knife?

                                            I will take a knife if you wish it.

You must leave me.

                                            I'm supposed to love another?

You're supposed to love him.

VI.

Stories make men want war.
King Adrastus: "Tydeus has returned.
For us, this is enough.
To kill, we must think.
To think, we must ask."

The king calls his prophets.
Apollo's loves: Grandfather Melampus, Amphiaraus.
First the offal. Tripe, blood,
and then the sheep's hearts.
But no response is given.

They search the sky from
cliffs where Perseus tried flight.
Amphiaraus calls out for birds
who, either from inborn atoms,
or limbed now winged experience

or because Jupiter touches heaven
touches sky or, simply, because
so few hours are spent
on heavy earth they know
the time known by gods.

If war: birds, sing victory
and bring us bright thunder.
If nothing: birds, be silent,
darken the sky with bodies.
Two prophets in tuneless harmony.

Suddenly birds of prey screeching
and hooting owls and laughter.
A dumb crow's mindless caw.
Hear nothing but unvirtuous noise.
Amphiaraus remembers nothing worse, nothing.

VII.

Seven swans appear silently standing
in a circle like guards
paid to do nothing but
watch for signs from elsewhere.
Seven eagles carrying thunderbolts land.

Opposite circle around circle rotates,
each bird dies in congress,
and our attempts to ask,
to see, are proven careless
and absurd, lonely, and unforgiven.

VIII.

Now speech follow speech
one voice become four,
yeast wants the flour,
singers want their scores.

None who sing know
how sound is heard
but light lights light
and night brings sight.

So sing their attempts,
Marion, Julia, William, and Mike,
and give song sense,
let words read right.

IX.

The Lovers' Song

She will tell you, and then this little speech will end.
  In this how little the little bird cries under the moon.
Late night limits, how it limits, what it limits.
  Violent sickness—I had fevers in the spring and fall.
Ending with no hesitance, the march for love.
  Reserved, alone, I would never position "the world."

Rising, I've never fallen, but I've used gravity, if you get my drift.
  Only what the hawk provides, the camaraderie of flight.
Send forward the moments of congruence, metaphysics.
  Either containment, or I made nothing of myself except sweet chatter.

X.

See by lamplight Garcia's wooden bedside table, the red book read until darkness comes. Book XIII, double vision twins language:

sunt viridi prato confinia litora, quorum
    There is a shore fringed by verdant meadows
altera pars undis, pars altera cingitur herbis,
    one side hemmed by waves, the other, vegetation

Then memories of youthful sadism fueled by *The Art of Love*
interrupt the barreling verse. An imagined performance piece,
only conceived, never presented, of a man in Hollywood
director pastiche, 1920s, yelling in Latin through a
megaphone at a crisp starlet attempting to follow the rules:

Sint modici rictus, parvaeque utrimque lacunae,
    Let the mouth be but moderately opened, let the dimples be small
et summos dentes ima labella tangent.
    and let the bottom of the lip cover the top of the teeth.

Only in the face of such struggle for form, his fundamental
self would have argued, could our chains be dissolved with dialectics
leading, of course, for a boy that age, to utopian fucking.
Imagined means lost to time, real ends known then in dark rooms now
only exist in imagination, dreams, nothing but the book.

quae postquam rediit, alium me corpore toto,
    When my senses came back to me, I was far different
ac fueram nuper, neque eundem mente recepi:
    from what I was but lately in all my body, nor was my mind the same.
hanc ego tum primum viridem ferrugine barbam
    Then for the first time I beheld this beard of dark green hue,
caeseriemque meam, quam longa per aequora verro,
    these locks which sweep on the long waves,
ingentesque umeros et caerula bracchia vidi
    these huge shoulders and bluish arms,
cruraque pinnigero curvata novissima pisce.
    these legs which twist and vanish in a finny fish.

XI.

The Dialogue of the Two Twins

She will tell you, and then this little speech will end.
In this how little the little bird cries under the moon.
Late night limits, how it limits, what it limits.
Violent sickness—I had fevers in the spring and fall.
Ending with no hesitance, the march for love.
Reserved, alone, I would never position "the world."

Rising, I've never fallen, but I've used gravity, if you get my drift.
Only what the hawk provides, the camaraderie of flight.
Send forward the moments of congruence, metaphysics.
Either containment, or I made nothing of myself except sweet chatter.

XII.

quid tamen haec species, quid dis placuisse marinis,
        and yet, what boots this form, what, that I pleased the sea-gods
quid iuvat esse deum, sit u non tangeris istis?
        what profits it to be a god if you are not moved by these things?

XIII.

That we might only love
earth and the love next
to us as airy nothings
instead of chasing solid power.
For now, as always, war.

XIV.

Flickering Bacchus sees soldiers moving
against his lovers, unready Thebes,
so he dries Earth's rivers.
Dust without and fever within,
the line becomes a circle

but the soldiers find nothing,
no water high or low.
Only then Hypsipyle is seen,
Opheltes, Lycurgus's son on hip.
King Adrastus calls her Diana.

He asks her for water.
Many Theban heads in return.
She is not a goddess
but she knows a secret
underground river Bacchus left alone.

XV.

Deray, Kieron, each with open tallboy climb The Complex's steps.
Soon, it will begin, that outdoor party you've heard of or been to
where the only limit is time, of which there is always enough,
and where space, body, and mind become desire's invisible force.
What did you wear, how does the cloth feel touching your body?
What did you think, how does it feel to remember?
Who will you touch again,
who will you touch instead?

XVI.

Inside the earth Langia flows.
The crying child set down,
flowers piled all around him.
When they leave, he stirs
to wander through the forest.

Then they run through dark
greens hiding in darker greens.
See finally running blue water
into which all who dive
are indiscriminate: humans, horses, chariots.

One body moving without reason.
Each finding underneath their body
something muddier until, through them,
all colors mix into darkness.
The wandering forest child dies.

Vol. 3: The Body
Argument

A Party at The Complex—Tisiphone Loosens Tigers, War Begins—Luke Djs, Soldiers Die—Gilberto and Jesse are Lovers—Kieron Rips His Jeans—William Changes, Soldiers Die—Eve and Ted Bring Reinforcements—Mike Sings Along to Pharoahe Monch—Amphiaraus, the Seer—Julia Sits—Apollo takes over for Amphiaraus, Soldiers Die—Geoffrey and Katherine Grill—Abbie Sits, Chelsea Laughs, Evan Blushes, Deray Farts, Soldiers Die, William Kneels, Marion Hides, Apollo Keeps Going—Amphiaraus Regains Control—Earthquake!—Julia Leads Dancers Upstairs, William Leads Stoners Upstairs—Julia, Abbie, and Mike Dance—Marion, Alone—Amphiaraus Drives into the Earth, into the Underworld—Garcia Dreams, Marion Sees—Mike Requests Bangers—William, Marion, Nothing Said—Luke Plays 2 Live Crew—Mike Makes a Move—Julia Runs Down the Stairs, Jumps in the Pool—Pluto asks Amphiaraus how he should be Punished—Geoffrey Grinds Katherine—William Gets a Towel—Julia and Marion, Alone—Julia goes to William—Marion goes to Geoffrey and Katherine—Amphiaraus tells Pluto to Punish his Wife

I.

Now night's
seed light
expands
The Complex.

Four lovers
welcomed by
'70s pool

and a chorus
in
drinking contest.

Deray, Kieron,
Abbie, Chelsea,
Evan yell
incomprehensible words
that make
selfish actions
possible.

Closed eyes
see war.
Open them,
the same.

The battle
begins.

My hands
are full.

Merged groups
pass flasks.

Ecstasy's
the aim.

Tisiphone
loosens tigers.

II.

Luke,
above in 28,
opens door,
windows.

Positions speakers.
Begins spinning
double-voiced
Latyrx.

*Her interests
are all
limitless,
she ain't
limited by
inhibitions,
Lord.*

Sybaris's
silver
blade.

Pterelas's
shoulder,
thigh.

Ityx's
fast
arrow.

Deray's
raised
elbow.

Chelsea's
formal
nod,
lovesick.

When you enter
a room
and everyone
looks at you—

that, here,
reversed.

Transfixed,
we see
it all,

bodies
struck
still,

Texan,
Theban,
a dreaming
tragedian.

III.

Gilberto, Jesse
throw keys
at William
as they come
down stairs.

Their four eyes
wander,
four hands
smooth
hair.

Evan
raises
eyebrow
at Deray.
A prophecy
confirmed.

Knowledge of
new secret
coupling
silently
infects the
circle's
mind,

informs
an action:

Kieron,
drunken
high kick.

Tight
Levi's
rip
in the crotch.

Choral laughter
dissolves
any
potential
inquisition.

New lovers bum,
share a cigarette.

William,
keys in hand,
jogs up steps
to change.

"Do we need
more beer?"

"Yes,"
he shouts,
slams
his door.

IV.

Eunaeus's shield
is painted
with ivy.

Capneus's,
a hydra.
On his helmet,
a giant.

William removes
silver clothing,
puts on
second-best
hoodie.

A spear
moves
through
Eunaeus.

V.

Ted, Eve,
out of
costume,
enter.

Each,
a case.

No need for
a beer run.

Collect dollars
from all
present.

The night
begins
again.

Luke plays
Pharoahe Monch.

His words
meet
William scrubbed
red,
white,
and silver.

Mike sings,
proud,
pinched.
Ready
to accept
or deny:

*Girls
rub on
your titties.*

The seer,
Amphiaraus's
shield
is a python
lit
by a god.

VI.

Julia
collapses into
a deck chair.

William watches
Marion watch
Julia adjust
her blouse
while watching
Mike
who
is watching
himself hold
in
a cough
behind
the smoke
of
a gratuitous
inhalation
bragged
about
before done.

Unity
added
to infinity
does not
increase
at all.

Apollo
drives
Amphiaraus's
chariot.
The god
kills for
his seer.

VII.

Phlegyas
Phyleus
Clonis
Chremetaon
Chromis
Iphinous
Sages
Gyas
Lycoreus
Alcathous

Geoffrey,
on the patio
off 13,
worries
the coals,
shifts
the vegetables,
while Katherine
lists
her day.
Their love
is quiet,
free.
Slight changes
each notices
in the other
after the day's
separation
makes sound
without end.

Their moment
infinitive.
Our
imagination
so magnifies

the present,
so reduces
eternity.

VIII.

Abbie
sits,
too quickly.

Legs
winnow.

Chelsea
laughs,
Evan
blushes.

Abbie,
Julia,
two girls
reclining,
wait.

Apollo drives
his seer
towards
more slaughter.

The music
has changed:
Key
my brain.

Each self
distracted finds
communal negation.

Deray coughs
to hide
a fart.

IX.

Menelaus
Antiphus
Aëtion
Polites
Lampus

Suddenly,
space arranges
around Julia.

William
wobbily
kneels,
then falls
on his ass.

Their heads,
the same
level.

Marion,
phasing in
and out
of misanthropy
steps between
Mike
and
the new
couple.

Ghosts pursue
Apollo's chariot.
He looks at
his priest.
God cannot
help death.

Nature
diversifies,
artifice
imitates
and imitates.

Wisdom
literature
in
fashionable jeans.

X.

Amphiaraus takes
the reins
and now
the Earth
eases
into
its work.

Julia,
inveterate
laughter at
William's
sarcastic
self-hatred,
bubbles
reclining
nausea.

The married
couple sees
it all.
"Oof,
they just took
four shots
apiece."
"Jealous?"
"Oh sure,
I relish
my life
before you.
Cookies
for breakfast,
lunch.
Playing hooky
from work
to take
Xena to

the vet."
Julia's hand,
liquid
silver
vibration,
grabs
air.

The surface
quakes,
internal rumbles
rumble.

This is
another noise
of war
and everything
lowers:
arms,
soldiers,
horses,
leafy
heights,
walls.

All hear,
feel,
an earthquake.

XI.

Marion,
now joined
to Mike,
at first,
double listening.

Suddenly,
the world
disappears
and vision
joins
her body.

An inward
drift
finally clear
to Marion,
as Julia,
having
found Abbie
in her wild
flailing,
escapes her body's
internal
retching through
redirection.

Those interested
follow Julia
upwards.

Marion sits,
still,
alone.

The river escapes,
anger perishes,

spears
are fixed
in the ground,
useless.

XII.

On the balcony,
a choice.
William
tries to lead
stoners
to his
apartment,
thinking Julia
will follow.

Instead,
she leads
Abbie into
Luke's room.
Mike follows.
Moves things
indiscriminately.

Dancing
begins.

William,
follow through,
retrieves
a bubbler.

Marion,
still,
alone.

All recede
into
themselves.

XIII.

No voice
but Marion's,
for Marion,
and love
indefinite
finds
its purpose.

No world
but
her world.

Either earth
dreamed wind,
or land
consumed itself
with underground
waves
or maybe sky
moved its stars and
so shifted
sea or
simply all
Nature
loved Apollo's
seer so
the chasm opens.

Chthonic man drives
horses safely into
the dirt
and he finally
looks up
as
the earth closes,
bringing sight
inwards.

XIV.

Garcia's Dream

I dreamed this was the primeval forest.
The earth's green hands slurred my vision
to re-dampen dream's time from its source.
In the darkness, I learned to listen—
Do not interrupt, I must tell someone
how I heard, and in hearing saw
what was without within. —This isn't London,
I am the chorus, I am law,
we are backstage warming up, dressed
in glitter and felt and feathers. Lights
and the curtain. So begins the quest:
I am the follies on opening night.
The thigh kicks the leg, the foot
silences the body, off comes the suit.

XV.

Silence the body, off comes the suit.
The blocking turns us into each other.
A line becomes a circle. The flute
calls us. In step we move further
upstage until no one, no individual appears
to me, my self in the audience.
What odd sympathy! Two crowds. One tiered
on stage, the other attending. This congruence
charges my division my body two bodies
plural who feel in two ways difference's
accordance as my follies show ancient follies
how measured geometric movement once became illiterate.
To restore sight, restore the symbol's dance.
Reveal the knife, show us the lance.

XVI.

Marion's Vision

Reveal the knife, show us the lance.
The Complex softens with his movement away
from me and in this my chance.
Three bodies, two on stage in foreplay
and I become other, my self the witness
that sees itself in two who dally
and see no self but two fearless
to progress from curtain to the finale.
My mind attends my heart's ascendant objective
with wrath, and shame, and Ladies sake.
Soon I will ascend from this collective,
transform my three selves into someone opaque.
A curtain call for novel, discreet nature
now lonely on stage, looking at strangers.

XVII.

Now, lonely on stage looking at strangers
centered vision opens wisdom's moment upwards
in new natural movement: SHRUB SEEDS LIGHT TEENAGERS.
Earth springs silver exhalations not dawn words.
Matter, ring! I strike the five hammers
with my five hands in five gloves,
I find the vicarious in objects' glamours,
I am Lilith who gives away love
so that my music, my sounds forge
not itself/object nor singular subject's splendor
but strange harmony. Not birch, allegheny spurge
I have grown with a moving center
a spangled vibration. I strike the inchus
and see one consonance that links us.

XVIII.

One in
the booth,
three on
the floor.

Without
explosive bangers Mike
is useless.

The girls'
subtle movement
keeps the room
from spinning.

Mike
looks at
Luke.

DJs
know this
overbearing proposal,

that
help-a-guy-in-need
plea.

William watches
Marion
from above.

Falling Amphiauraus misses
purification
and marking.

Corpses marvel
at the sweat
on his body

and then
his body.

XIX.

Marion sees
William approach.

"Our lonely couple…"
Katherine gestures.
She knows
less than Geoffrey.
"Not anymore,
I don't think."

He works
from home.
He overhears
gossip.

He'd found
a new way
through Earth into
the underworld.

Pluto
is forced
to see stars and,
unable to hate
their light
curses the world.

2 Live Crew
stains
The Complex.

XX.

Julia,
red-faced,
loose stomach,
storms down the stairs,
jumps clothed
into
the pool.

The splash keeps
old lovers from
speaking.

Geoffrey:
"Interesting choice."
"What?"
"The music."

His happiness
never denies
movement.

XXI.

Pluto:
"Tisiphone builds monsters."

Geoffrey's hand
around his wife's
still
waist.

"Brothers kill brothers."

Tongs up,
snap, snap.

"Heroes cannibalize heroes."

Grinds her.
Nasty as
she lets
him be.

"You, you there.
How should I punish you?"

A young old man out of breath.

"You think you're sooo funny."

XXII.

Self-dunked Julia escapes
Mike's body
and
her body.

Marion
suspects drama
as
she surfaces.

William
plays
his part.

In
his apartment's
a
moldy towel
he keeps
for guests.

As she climbs out
he runs
to get it.

"Where'd everybody
go?"
the dripping
girl
asks
the girl
responsible.

The two whisper
unaware
of the moments
shared.

The mind
is blind,
cloned.

The body
is dumb,
attended
by no one
or
only
one
doubled.

Doubled
space
is wasted
time.

How metaphor
is
refused.

XXIII.

"Up here!"
William shouts,
towel
in hand.

"Oh good."
Marion watches
Julia leave.

Luke,
the DJ,
watches Abbie, Mike,
give new meaning
to old song.

William
sees Julia
loosely dry
her arms,

wrap her golden hair
in a red towel.

Geoffrey watches
Katherine wave
Marion over.

Warmth given
to younger self.

The couple greets Marion.
Asks no questions about
this poem's moment.
Instead,
ask her to
measure her present
momentum.

Their wedding's allowance:

no doubt.
"Um...
I've been thinking about..."

The director
becomes
a performer.

XXIV.

Amphiaraus:
"If holy men can speak here,
in the underworld,
I,
who know cause
and cause's cause,
will speak.

I accept fate
though I've done nothing
for it.
My wife brought me
into war.

And now,
swallowed by earth,
earth
is without me,
without
my ashes.
I
am content.

I loved ghosts
in life,
tried to see them,
learned to read them,
and now
my body
becomes one
with them.
For me,
there's no punishment
here.
Punish
my wife."

A Note on the Text

For my adaptation of Statius's *Thebaid* I relied on two translations as lodestones: Jane Wilson Joyce's translation from Cornell, and J. H. Mozley's translation in the Loeb edition. Joyce's gloss of names was also especially helpful. I've attempted to move my adaptation beyond these translators' tutelage, but I no doubt internalized many of their choices and interpretations as I worked towards my own version of the myth. I'd like this book to be thought of as an interlocutor to their translations, and that any credit for comprehension of Statius and his poem might be redirected back to their work.

Devin King is the poetry editor of the Green Lantern Press and the author of *CLOPS*, *The Resonant Space*, and *These Necrotic Ethos Come the Plains*.

KENNING EDITIONS

Juana I, by Ana Arzoumanian, translated by Gabriel Amor

Waveform, by Amber DiPietra and Denise Leto

Style, by Dolores Dorantes, translated by Jen Hofer

PQRS, by Patrick Durgin

The Pine-Woods Notebook, by Craig Dworkin

Propagation, by Laura Elrick

Tarnac, a preparatory act, by Jean-Marie Gleize, translated by Joshua Clover with Abigail Lang and Bonnie Roy

Stage Fright: Selected Plays from San Francisco Poets Theater, by Kevin Killian

The Kenning Anthology of Poets Theater: 1945-1985, edited by Kevin Killian and David Brazil

Insomnia and the Aunt, by Tan Lin

The Compleat Purge, by Trisha Low

Ambient Parking Lot, by Pamela Lu

Some Math, by Bill Luoma

Partisan of Things, by Francis Ponge, translated by Joshua Corey and Jean-Luc Garneau

The Dirty Text, by Soleida Ríos, translated by Barbara Jamison and Olivia Lott

The Pink, by Kyle Schlesinger

Who Opens, by Jesse Seldess

Left Having, by Jesse Seldess

Grenade in Mouth: Some Poems of Miyó Vestrini, edited by Faride Mereb and translated by Anne Boyer and Cassandra Gillig

Hannah Weiner's Open House, by Hannah Weiner, edited by Patrick Durgin

Kenningeditions.com